ELTON JOHN DUETS

Piano/Vocal/Guitar

teardrops · 8

when I think about love (I think about you) · 18

the power · 24

shakey ground · 32

true love · 38

if you were me · 45

a woman's needs · 52

old friend · 60

go on and on · 67

don't go breaking my heart · 77

ain't nothing like the real thing · 86

i'm your puppet · 92

love letters · 98

born to lose · 104

don't let the sun go down on me · 111

duets for one · 119

Folio © 1994 International Music Publications Limited
Southend Road, Woodford Green, Essex IG8 8HN
Music Transcribed by Barnes Music Engraving Ltd., East Sussex TN22 4HA
Front & Back Cover Photos by Brian Aris
Printed by Panda Press · Haverhill · Suffolk CB9 8PR
Reproducing this music in any form is illegal and forbidden
by the Copyright, Designs and Patents Act 1988.

215-2-1160

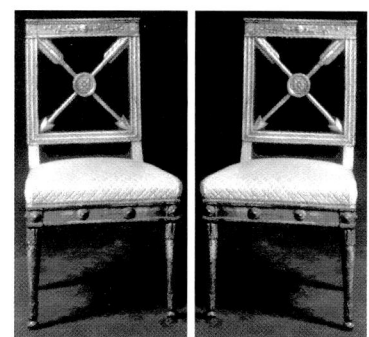

k.d. lang
& Elton John

tear drops

P.M. Dawn
& Elton John

*when I think
about love
(I think about you)*

Little Richard
& Elton John

the power

Don Henley
& Elton John

shakey ground

Kiki Dee
& Elton John

true love

Chris Rea
& Elton John

if you were me

Tammy Wynette
& Elton John

a woman's needs

George Michael
& Elton John

*don't let the sun
go down on me*

Nik Kershaw
& Elton John

old friend

Gladys Knight
& Elton John

go on and on

RuPaul
& Elton John

*don't go breaking
my heart*

Marcella Detroit
& Elton John

*ain't nothing like
the real thing*

Paul Young & Elton John
I'm your puppet

Bonnie Raitt & Elton John
love letters

Leonard Cohen & Elton John
born to lose

Elton John
duets for one

Teardrops

Whenever I hear goodbye
(Reminds me baby of you)
I break down and cry
(The next time I'll be true yeah)
Fever for lost romance
(Reminds me baby of you)
I took a crazy chance
(The next time I'll be true I'll be true)

Footsteps on the dance floor
(Remind me baby of you)
Teardrops in my eyes
(The next time I'll be true yeah)
Whispers in the back room
(She cries on every tune every tune . . .)

And the music don't feel like it did
When I felt it with you
Nothing that I do or feel
Ever feels like I felt it with you

When I'm dancing 'round
(Reminds me baby of you)
I won't let you down
(The next time I'll be true I'll be true)

Footsteps on the dance floor
(Remind me baby of you)
Teardrops in my eyes
(The next time I'll be true yeah)
Whispers in the back room
(She cries on every tune every tune)

Whenever I hear goodbye
(Reminds me baby of you)
I break down and cry
(Next time I'll be true, I'll be true)

And the music don't feel like it did
When I felt it with you
Nothing that I do or feel
Ever feels like I felt it with you

And the music don't feel like it did
When I felt it with you
Nothing that I do or feel
Ever feels like I felt it with you

Teardrops

Music & Lyrics by
ZEKKARIYAS/ZERIIYA ZEKKARIYAS

© 1988 Next Flight Music
(Administered by Zomba Music Publishers Ltd. For the UK & Eire) NW10 2SG

When I Think About Love
(I Think About You)

Holding all the pictures that my life's drawn
I never find I'm missing love
Remembering all parades that had been rained on
But never cloudy leaving love

Ask me what it is that makes it special
Why it's so real to me
It's knowing who keeps their place in my heart
It's knowing how is it I can feel you
It's knowing never will I change my mind

When I think about love, I think about you girl
When I think about love, I think about you

Too many times I've turned my emotions on and off
Without realising what it does
I know what's moved me and kept me going this far
But I never questioned what it was

Ask me what it is that makes it special
Why it's so real to me
It's knowing who keeps their place in my heart
It's knowing how is it I can feel you
It's knowing never will I change my mind

When I think about love, I think about you girl
When I think about love, I think about you girl
When I think about love, I think about you

So ask me what it is that makes it special
Makes it special and why it's so real to me
It's knowing knowing who keeps their place in my heart
It's knowing how is it I can feel you
It's knowing never will I change my mind

When I think about love, I think about you
When I think about love
When I think about love, I think about you

The Power

I have sold myself through and through
I have walked in the darkness too
Felt a red sun the living proof
Washed my hands in the honest truth
I have carried this weight time after time
I have battled the dumb and the blind
I've seen dignity fail and colours run
Seen justice denied by the voice of a gun

And we walk yes we walk
And we walk with the power every day
Never letting the light slip away
Reaching out reaching in
Touching truth and touching skin
Never letting the light slip away
And we walk with the power every day

If my faith is a fire then burn baby burn
We've held fire long enough to learn
Heat beneath hope is a healing light
Kept alive by the flames of night
Walk tall in the power day after day
And never never never lose sight of the way
See the dawn come and the dusk hang
See the power rise from an open hand

And we walk and we walk with the power every day
Never letting the light slip away
Reaching out reaching in
Touching truth and touching skin
Never letting the light slip away
And we walk with the power every day

Yeah we walk
Yeah yeah yeah we walk yeah we walk
Yes we walk with the power every day
Never letting the light slip away
Reaching out reaching in
Touching truth and touching skin
Never letting the light slip away
And we walk with the power every day

Walk walk with the power
Walk with the power walk walk

THE POWER

Music by ELTON JOHN
Lyrics by BERNIE TAUPIN

© 1993 Happenstance Ltd./Hania
Administered by Warner Chappell Music Ltd., London W1Y 3FA

SHAKEY GROUND

Lady Luck and four-leaf clovers
Won't ease this hurt I feel all over
My life was one special occasion
Till your leaving dampened the situation

Well well well
Standing on shakey ground
Ever since you put me down
Standing on shakey ground
Ever since you put me down

My car got repossessed this morning
Harder times I haven't seen in years
Girl you'd better throw me a life preserver
'Cause I'm about to drown in my own tears

Well well well
Standing on shakey ground
Ever since you put me down
Standing on shakey ground
Ever since you put me down

Well well well
Standing on shakey ground
Ever since you put me down
Standing on shakey ground
Ever since you put me down

Shakey Ground

Music & Lyrics by
JEFFREY BOWEN, EDDIE HAZEL
& ALPHONSO BOYD

La-dy Luck and four-leaf clo-vers won't ease this hurt I feel all
My car got re-pos-sessed this morn-ing, hard-er times I have-n't seen in

o - ver.
years.
My life was one spe-cial oc-ca-sion,
Girl, you'd bet-ter throw me a life pre-ser-ver,

© 1974 Jobete Music Co., Inc./Stone Diamond Music Corp., USA
Sub-published by Jobete Music (U.K.) Ltd., London WC2H 0EA

36

True Love

Sun-tanned, wind-blown
Honeymooners at last alone
Feeling far above par
Oh how lucky we are

While I give to you
And you give to me
True love true love
So on and on it will always be
True love true love

For you and I have a guardian angel
On high with nothing to do
But to give to you
As you give to me
Love forever true
Love forever true

True Love

Music & Lyrics by
COLE PORTER

Sun-tanned, wind-blown, hon-ey-moon-ers at last a-lone, feel-ing far a-bove par, oh how luc-ky we

© 1956 Cole Porter Music/Buxton Hill Music Corp./
Administered by Warner Chappell Music Ltd., London W1Y 3FA

are. While I give to you, and you give to me, true love, true love, so on and on it will always be true love, true love. For you and I have a guardian an-gel on high, with no-thing to do, but to give to you, as you give to me, love for-ev-er

41

true love, oh yeah, oh yeah, true love, true love. For you and I have a guardian angel on high, with nothing to do, but to give to you, as you give to me, love for-ev-er true, love for-ev-er true, love for-ev-er true love.

If You Were Me

If you were me
And I was you
If you had to play my part out
What would you do?
Two crazy stories
Two different views
If you were me
And I was you

If you were me and I was you
What kind of crazy things
Would I have to do?
Who likes to party?
Who stays at home
If you were me
And I was you?

Never like strangers
Though never the same
Two circus side shows
That laughed in the rain
You stayed with the full moon
You searched for the stars
Thank God in his heaven
Here we both are

If you were me
And I was you
If you had to play my part out
What would you do?
Two crazy stories
Two different views
If you were me
If you were me
If you were me
And I was you

If you were me
And I was you
If you were me
And I was you

If You Were Me

Music & Lyrics by
CHRIS REA

(♩ = 96)

If you were me, ___ and I was you, ___
If you were me, ___ and I was you, ___

if you had to play ___ my part ___ out, what would you do? ___
what kind of cra- zy things ___ would I have to do? ___

© 1993 Navybeck Ltd./Magnet Music Ltd., London W1Y 3FA

B♭7
C/G
Caug5/G♯
2fr
Two cra - zy sto - ries,
Who likes to par - ty?
Am
F
Em7
Dm7
two dif - ferent views,
Who stays at home,
if you were me,
if you were me,
G
F/G
1.
C
G7/B
Am7
C/G
F
C/E
Dm
and I was you.
and I was you?
F/G
2.
B♭9
E♭
Ne-ver like stran -

-gers, though ne-ver the same,___ two cir-cus side-

-shows___ that laughed in the rain.___

You stayed with the full___ moon, you searched for the stars,

thank God in his hea-ven, here we

both are.

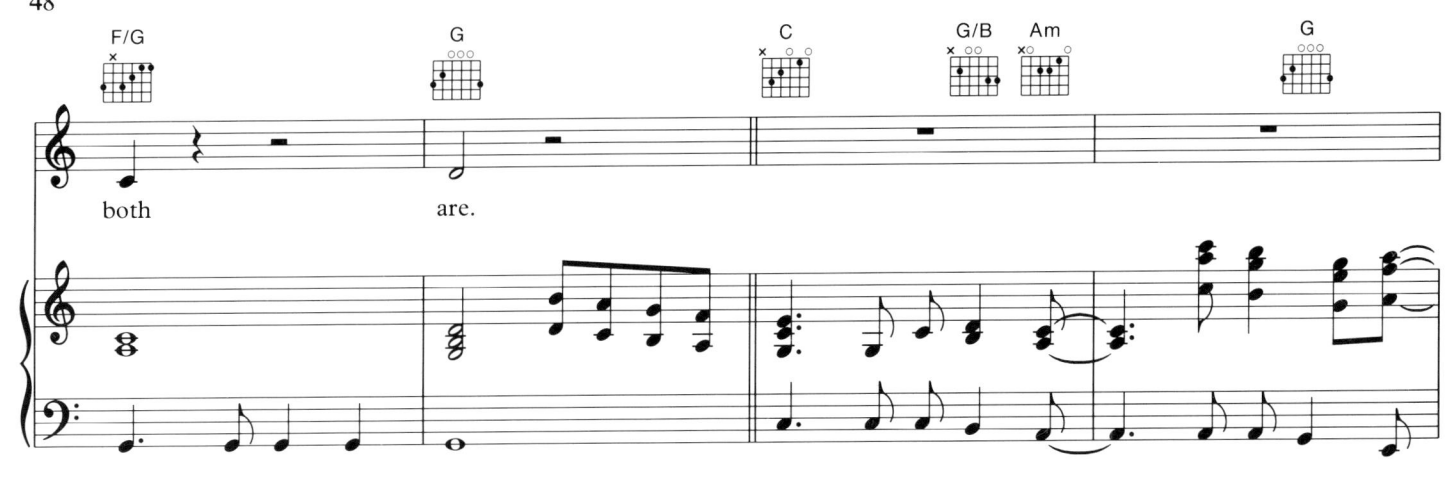

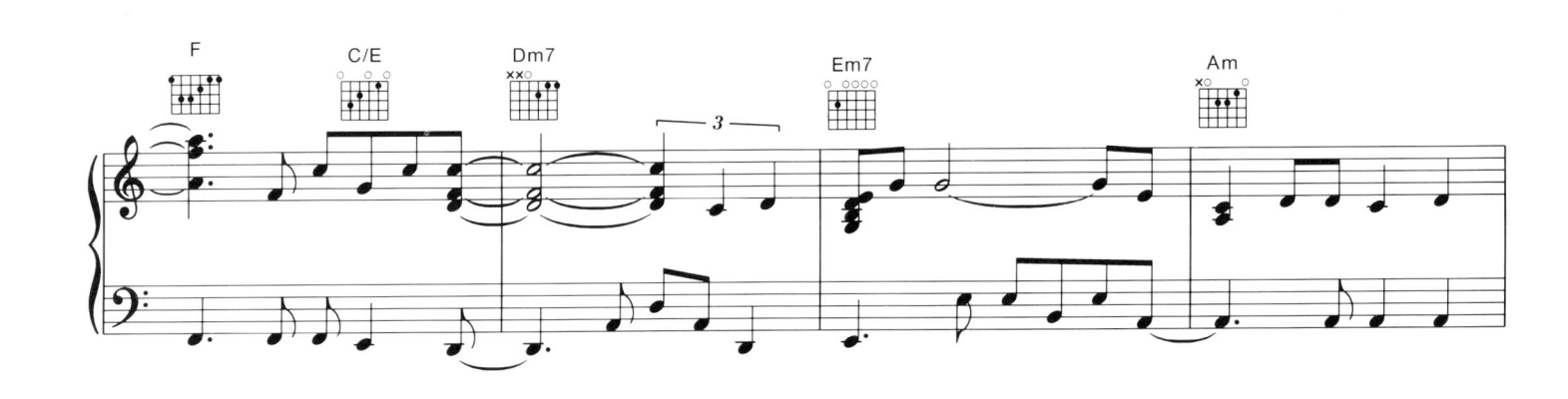

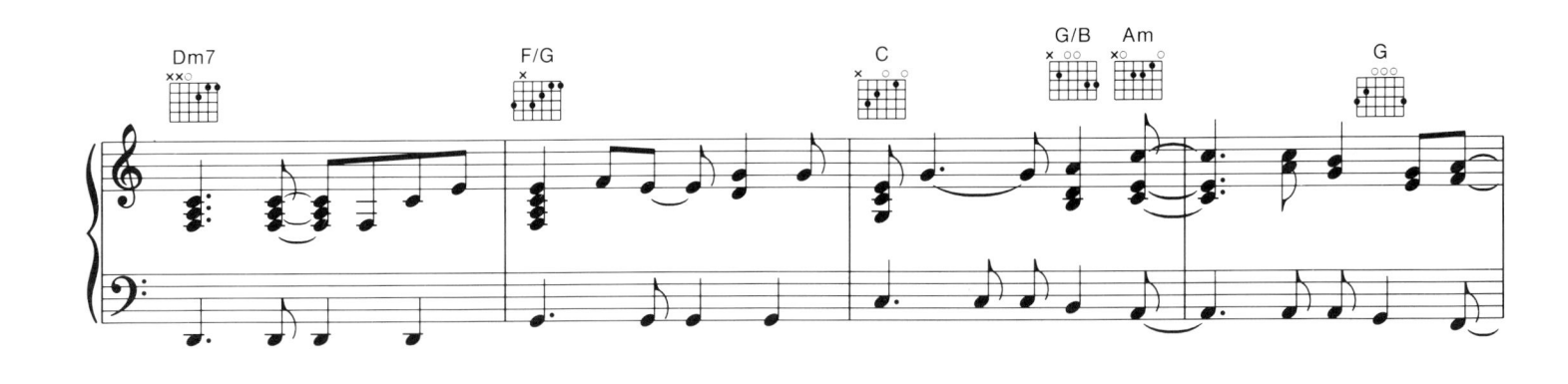

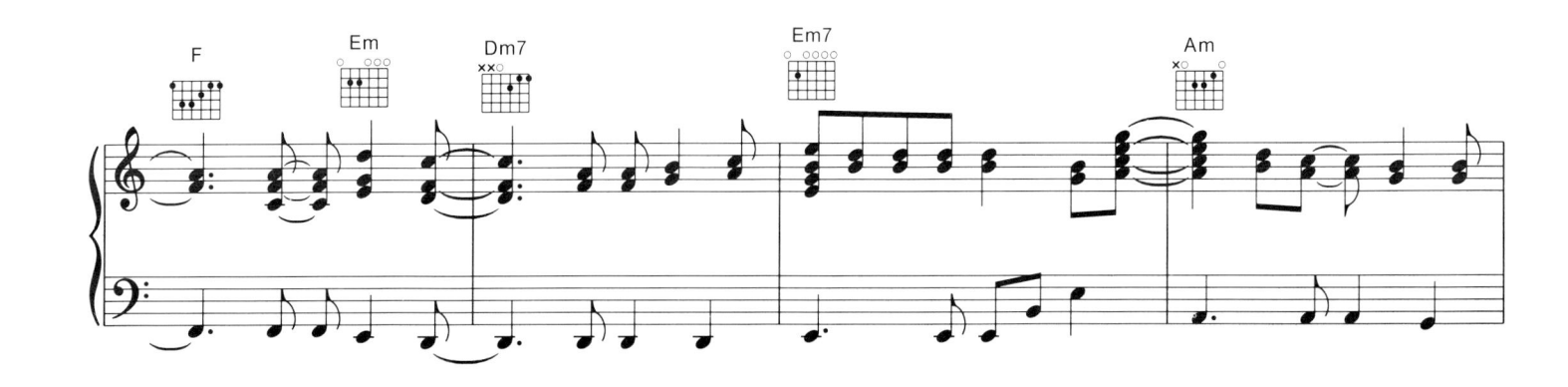

Lyrics:

If you were me, and I was you, if you had to play my part out, what would you do? Two crazy stories, two different views, if you were me, *if you were me,* _____ *if you were me,* _____

and I was you. _____ *If you were me,*

and I _____ *was you,* _____ *if you were me,*

and I _____ *was you.* _____

A Woman's Needs

Where have you been, are you still on my side?
Is that love or regret that I see in your eyes?
How many years have we played out this game?
Every time we come close the answer's always the same

I guess some souls get restless under the skin
There's a shortage by half of marrying men
You know that I love you but I love to be free
So tell me what do you want yeah from a gypsy like me?

I need a ring on my finger, champagne on ice
One man to show me the best part of life
Is that what you want?
Yeah that's what I need
A home and a family makes sense for us
A solid foundation built out of trust
Do you think you can find that with someone like me?
Two arms to hold you
One place to be
Are just some of the things that a woman needs

I've been short-changed and cheated so many times
But you're all that I've wanted for all of my life
I've searched for the reasons, known how I felt
But what can I give you when I can't trust myself?

I need a ring on my finger, champagne on ice
One man to show me the best part of life
Is that what you want?
Yeah that's what I need
A home and a family makes sense for us
A solid foundation built out of trust
Do you think you can find that with someone like me?
Two arms to hold you
One place to be
Are just some of the things that a woman needs

Two arms to hold you
One place to be
Are just some of the things that a woman needs
Two arms to hold you
One place to be
Are just some of the things that a woman needs

A Woman's Needs

Music by ELTON JOHN
Lyrics by BERNIE TAUPIN

(♩ = 126)

(She): Where have you been? _____ Are you
(He): I guess some souls get rest-less
(She): I've been short-changed, and cheat-ed

still on my side? _____
un-der the skin. _____
so ma-ny times,

© 1993 Happenstance Ltd./Hania
Administered by Warner Chappell Music Ltd., London W1Y 3FA

Is that love or re - gret,
There's a short - age by half
but you're all that I've want - ed

that I see in your eyes?
of mar - ry - ing men.
for all of my life.

How ma - ny
You know that I love you,
(*He*): I've searched for the rea - sons,

years
have we played out this
but I love to be
known how I

54

-ger, champagne on ice, one man to show me the best part of life. *(He):* Is it that what you want? *(She):* Yeah, that's what I need.

(Both): A home and a fam-

F
Dm
4fr
- ily makes sense for us, (She): a so - lid foun -
Gm
Cm
- da - tion, built out of trust. (He): Do you think you can find
F
Dm
4fr
that with some-one like me? (She): Two arms to hold
G7
Cm
you, one place to be, are just some of the things,

that a wo - man needs.

D.%. al Coda

needs.

(He): Two arms to hold you, one place to be, (She): are just some of the things, that a wo - man needs. *(He):* Two arms to hold you, one place to be, *(She):* are just some of the things, that a wo-man needs.

OLD FRIEND

I want to be good, I want to be strong
But I treated him bad, I've done him wrong
I've taken his money, I've given him hell
And he takes it all 'cause he knows me well

We can say what we mean and mean what we say
We don't like to mess around
But we're there to pull each other up when we've fallen down

Just like an old friend
Putting me on my feet again
Giving me back my pride then
Letting me go
Just like an old friend
Putting me in my place again
Giving me back my hope then
Letting me know
That he's an old friend

I don't suffer no fools, I've testified
But he must be one for being by my side
I've broken his heart, I've shaken his tree
But still he doesn't want anything from a fool like me

We won't talk for a year or two, maybe when we do
We won't say much
Even so, we know that out of mind is never out of touch

Just like an old friend
Putting me on my feet again
Giving me back my pride then
Letting me know
That he's an old friend

We're having a man to man
Don't want to get sentimental
But both of us understand
We'll never have to say goodbye
Just see you later

Just like an old friend
Putting me on my feet again
Giving me back my pride then
Letting me go
Just like an old friend
Putting me in my place again
Giving me back my hope then
Letting me know
Just like an old friend

Old Friend

Music & Lyrics by
NIK KERSHAW

($\quarter = 94$)

I want to be good, I want to be strong, but I treated him bad, I've done him wrong. I've

suffer no fools, I've testified, but he must be one for being by my side. I've

© 1993 Nik Kershaw

ta-ken his mon-ey, I've giv-en him hell, and he
bro-ken his heart, I've sha-ken his tree, but still he does-n't

takes it all,___ 'cause he knows me well. We can say___
want a-ny-thing from a fool like me. We won't talk___

___ what we mean, and mean___ what we say, we don't like to mess a-round,
___ for a year or two,___ may-be when we do,___ we won't say much.__

but we're there___ to pull each oth-er up when we've fall-en down.
Ev-en so___ we know that out of mind is ne-ver out of touch.

62

Just like an old friend, putting me on my feet again, giving me back my pride, then letting me go, just like an old friend, putting me in my place again, giving me back my hope,

— then letting me know, that he's an old friend.

I don't letting me know, that he's an old friend.

We're having a man to man, don't want to get sentimen-

-tal, but both of us un-der-stand we'll ne-ver have to say good-bye, just see you la-ter.

Just like an

old friend, putting me on my feet again, giving me back my pride, then letting me go, just like an old friend, putting me in my place again, giving me back my hope, then letting me know, just like an

repeat to fade

Go On And On

She broke my heart, he hurt me too
That's something that only unworthy souls would do
They say goodbye, we say hello
An introduction for a perfect love to grow

Let's stop thinking 'bout the past and start thinking 'bout the future
So that love can go on and on
Let's stop thinking 'bout the past and start thinking 'bout the future
So that love can go on and on

She said she'd stay, he said that too
So sad when you find out your love has found a new
She made me cry, he made me weep
But life has love in store for us that's oh so sweet

Let's stop thinking 'bout the past and start thinking 'bout the future
So that love can go on and on
Let's stop thinking 'bout the past and start thinking 'bout the future
So that love can go on and on and on and on
On and on, love keep going on
On and on, tick tock, old love clock
On and on, love keep going on on and

It's time to say goodbye to crying eyes and broken dreams
And get back to the joy that to each other we will bring
That starts from summer love to last through autumn, winter, spring
Our hearts will sing, forever love

Let's stop thinking 'bout the past and start thinking 'bout the future
So that love can go on and on
Let's stop thinking 'bout the past and start thinking 'bout the future
So that love can go on and on
Let's stop thinking 'bout the past and start thinking 'bout the future
So that love can go on and on and on and on on and on on and on

GO ON AND ON

Music & Lyrics by
STEVIE WONDER

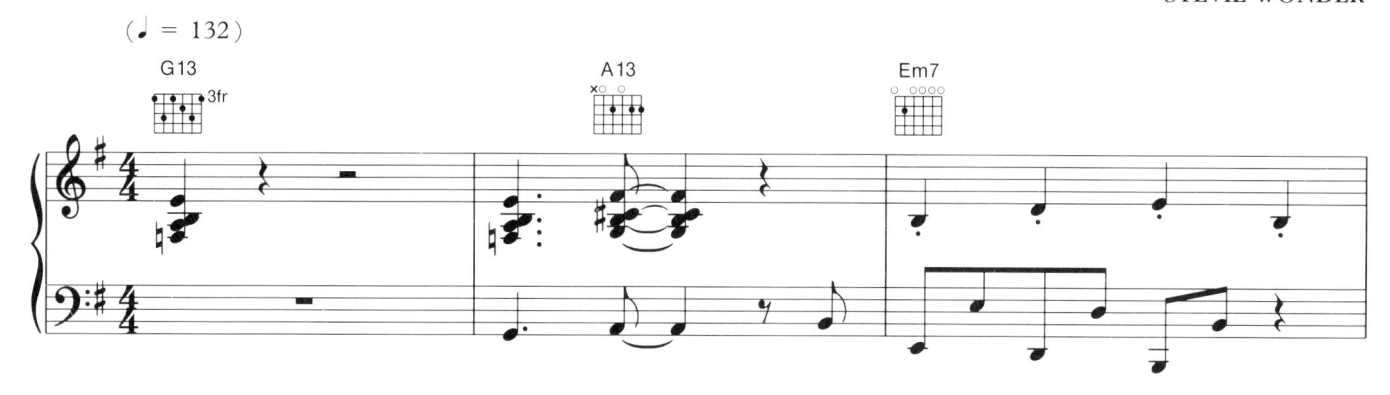

Lyrics:
On and on,

68

on and on.

(He): She broke my heart. (She): He hurt me too.
she'd stay. (She): He said that too.

(He): That's some-thing that on-ly un-wor-thy souls
(He): So sad when you find out your love has found

B7sus4/F
2fr
B
C/D
G
— would do. — They say — good - bye. — (She): We say —
— a - new. — She made — me cry. — (She): He made
G7
C
— hel - lo. — (Both): An in - tro - duc - tion for —
— me weep. — (Both): But life — has love — in store —
B7sus4/F
2fr
B7
— a per - fect love — to grow. —
— for us — that's oh — so sweet. —
Let's stop
Em
G
think - ing 'bout — the past, — and start think - ing 'bout — the fu -

-ture, so that love can go on and on.

Let's stop thinking 'bout the past, and start thinking 'bout the future, so that love can go on and on.

1.
and on. *(He):* She said

2.
Cm
3fr
Am
Cm
3fr
and on, and on, and on,
Em
G13
3fr
A13
Em7
on and on,
love keep go - ing on,
G13
3fr
A13
Em7
on and on, tick tock old

love clock, on and on, love keep going on, on and (He): It's time to say goodbye to crying eyes and broken dreams. (Both): And get back to the joy

that to each oth - er we will bring, ___ that starts from sum - mer love ___ to last ___ through au - tumn, win - ter, spring. ___ our hearts ___ will sing ___ for - ev - er love. ___ Let's stop think - ing 'bout ___ the past, ___ and start thinking 'bout the future, so that love can go on and on. Let's stop thinking 'bout the past, and start thinking 'bout the future, so that love can go on and on. Let's stop thinking 'bout the past,

and start thinking 'bout the future, so that love can go on and on, and on, and on.

On and on,

repeat to fade

on and on.

DON'T GO BREAKING MY HEART

Don't go breaking my heart
I couldn't if I tried
Oh honey if I get restless
Baby you're not that kind

Don't go breaking my heart
You take the weight off of me
Oh honey when you knocked on my door
I gave you my key

Ooh ooh nobody knows it
(Nobody knows it)
But when I was down
I was your clown
Ooh ooh nobody knows it
(Nobody knows it)
Right from the start
I gave you my heart
Oh oh I gave you my heart

So don't go breaking my heart
(Don't go breaking my)
I won't go breaking your heart
(Don't go breaking my don't go breaking my)
Don't go breaking my heart

And nobody told us
'Cause nobody showed us
And now it's up to us baby
Oh I think we can make it

So don't misunderstand me
You put the light in my life
Oh you put the spark to the flame
I've got your heart in my sights

Ooh ooh nobody knows it
(Nobody knows it)
But when I was down
I was your clown
Ooh ooh nobody knows it
(Nobody knows it)
Right from the start
I gave you my heart
Oh oh I gave you my heart

So don't go breaking my heart
(Don't go breaking my)
I won't go breaking your heart
(Don't go breaking my don't go breaking my)
Don't go breaking my heart

Ooh ooh
Nobody knows it
(Nobody knows it)
But when I was down
I was your clown
Right from the start
I gave you my heart
Oh oh I gave you my heart

Don't Go Breaking My Heart

Music & Lyrics by
ANN ORSON &
CARTE BLANCHE

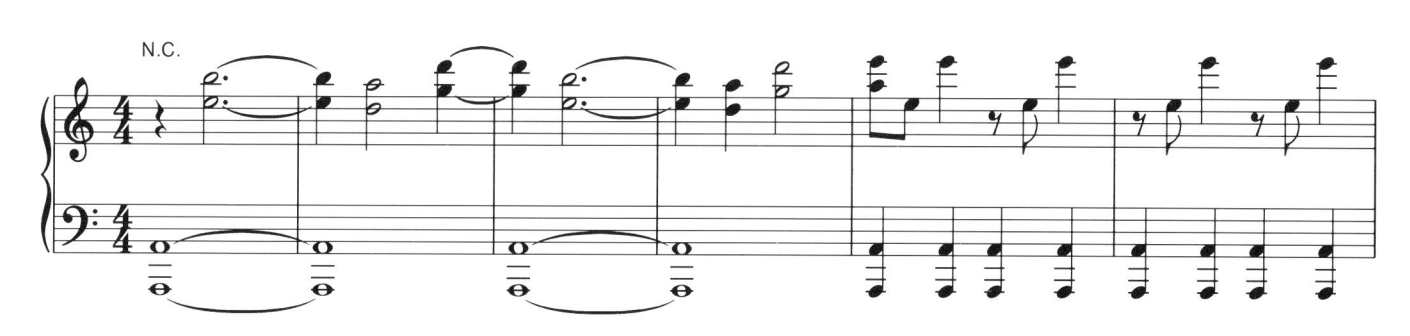

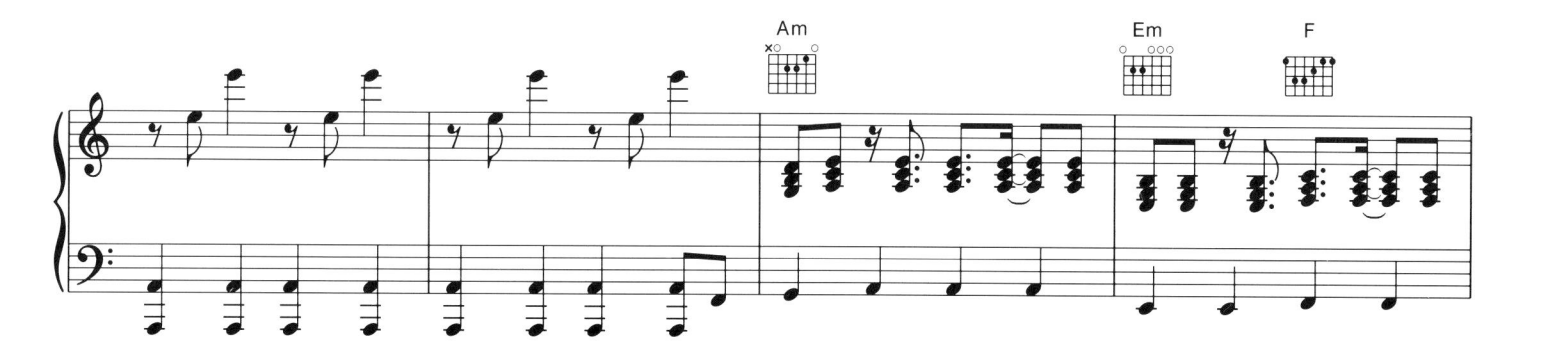

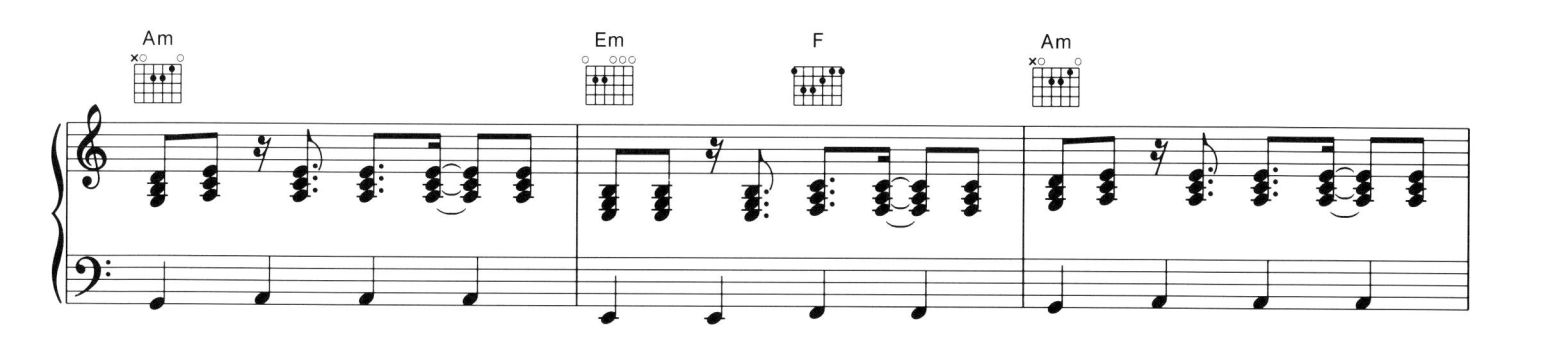

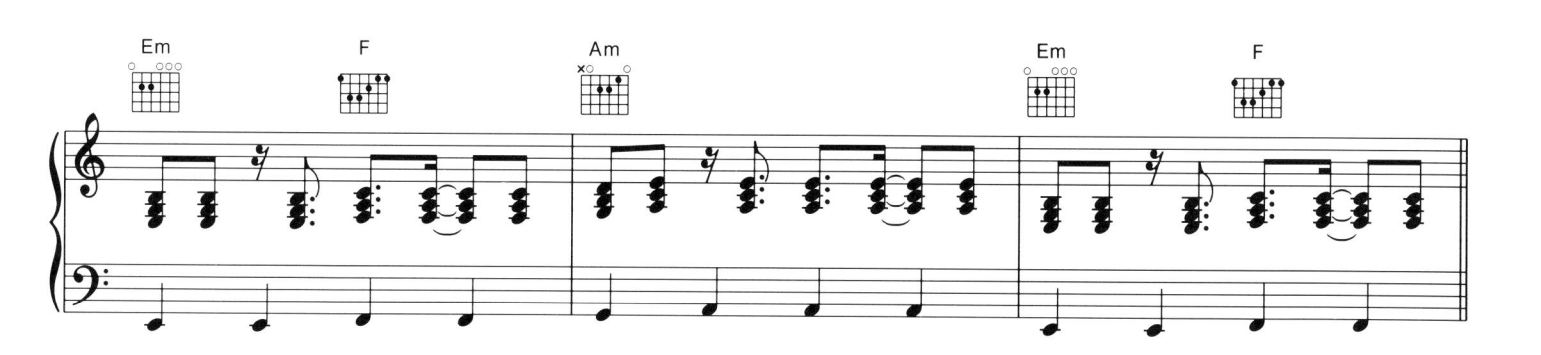

C
F
C
Don't go break-ing my heart,
I could-n't if I tried.
And no-bo-dy told us,
'cause no-bo-dy showed
F
C
E
F
D/F♯
Oh hon-ey, if I get rest-less,
us, and now it's up to us ba-by,
C/G
G
N.C.
ba-by, you're not that kind.
oh I think we can make it.
C
F
C
Don't go break-ing my heart,
you take the weight off me,
So don't mis-un-der-stand me,
you put the light in my life,

oh hon-ey, when you knocked on my door
oh, you put the spark to the flame,

I gave you my key.
I've got your heart in my sights.

Ooh, ooh, no-bo-dy knows it, (no-bo-dy knows

it,) but when I was down, I was your clown.

Ooh, ooh, no-bo-dy knows it, right from the start, I gave you my heart, oh, oh, I gave you my heart.

So don't go break-ing my heart, (don't go break-ing my,)

I won't go break-ing your heart, (don't go break-ing my, don't go break-ing my,) don't go break-ing my heart.

Mmm

Ooh, ooh, no-bo-dy knows it, (no-bo-dy knows it,) but when I was down, I was your clown, right from the start, I gave you my heart, ____ oh, ____ oh, ____ I gave you my heart. ____

So don't go break-ing my heart, ____ (don't go break-ing my,) I won't go break-ing your heart,

____ don't go break-ing my heart, ____ (don't go break-ing my,) I won't go break-ing your heart,

____ don't go break-ing my, don't go break-ing my, I won't go break-ing your heart.

Am
G/A
Dm/A
— Don't go break-ing my heart,
I won't go break-ing your heart,
Am
G/A
Dm/A
— don't go break-ing my heart.
I won't go break-ing your heart,
C
Am
F
G
— don't go break-ing my heart,
don't go break-ing my heart,
I won't go break-ing your heart,
C
Am
F
G
repeat to fade
— don't go break-ing my heart,
don't go break-ing my heart,
I won't go break-ing your heart.

Ain't Nothing Like
The Real Thing

Ain't nothing like the real thing baby
Ain't nothing like the real thing
Ain't nothing like the real thing baby
Ain't nothing like the real thing

I got your picture hanging on my wall
But it can't seem to come to me when I call your name
I realise it's just a picture in a frame
I read your letters but you're not here
They don't move me, they don't prove it like when I hear
Your sweet voice whispering in my ear

Ain't nothing like the real thing baby
Ain't nothing like the real thing
Ain't nothing like the real thing baby
Ain't nothing like the real thing

I play my games a fantasy
I've been down I don't see reality
I need the shelter of your arms to comfort me
I've got some memories to look back on
Though they help me when you're gone I'm well aware
Nothing can take the place of you being there
No other sound is quite the same as your name
No touch can do half as much to make me feel better
Let's stay together

Ain't nothing like the real thing baby
Ain't nothing like the real thing
Ain't nothing like the real thing baby
Ain't nothing like the real thing
I'm so so glad we got the real thing baby
So glad we got the real thing
Ain't nothing like the real thing baby
Ain't nothing like the real real real thing

Ain't Nothing Like The Real Thing

Music & Lyrics by
NICKOLAS ASHFORD &
VALERIE SIMPSON

© 1967 Jobete Music Co. Inc., USA
Sub-published by Jobete Music (U.K.) Ltd., London WC2H 0EA

picture hanging on my wall, but it can't sing or come to me when I
games, a fantasy, I've been down, I don't see re-
call your name, I realise it's just a picture in a frame. (*He*): I read your
-ality, I need the shelter of your arms to comfort me. (*He*): I've got some
letters, but you're not here, they don't move me, they don't prove it like
memories to look back on, though they help me when you're gone, I'm

1.
when I hear your sweet voice whispering in my ear, oh.
well aware nothing can take the place of your

being there, no other sound is quite the same as your name, no touch can do half as much to make me feel better. Let's stay together, ah, ah, ooh.

89

Ain't no-thing like the real thing ba - by, ain't no-thing like the

real, real, real thing.

fade

I'm Your Puppet

Pull the string and I'll wink at you
I'm your puppet
I'll do funny things if you want me to
I'm your puppet
I'm yours to have and to hold darling
You've got full control of your puppet

Pull another string and I'll kiss your lips
I'm your puppet
Snap your finger and I'll turn you some flips
I'm your puppet
Your every wish is my command
All you gotta do is wiggle your little hand
I'm your puppet
I'm your puppet

I'm just a toy just a funny boy
That makes you laugh when you're blue
I'll be wonderful do just what I'm told
I'll do anything for you
I'm your puppet
I'm your puppet

Pull them little strings and I'll sing you a song
I'm your puppet oh baby
Make me do right or make me do wrong
I'm your puppet
Treat me good and I'll do anything
I'm just a puppet and you hold my strings
I'm your puppet
Yeah I'm your puppet

Walking talking living loving puppet
I'm hanging on a string girl
I'll do anything now come on now
I'm your puppet
Walking, talking, living, loving, puppet
And I love you
I'm a smiling happy face when you want to
Even make you happy when you're feeling blue

I'm Your Puppet

Music & Lyrics by
LINDEN OLDHAM
& DAN PENN

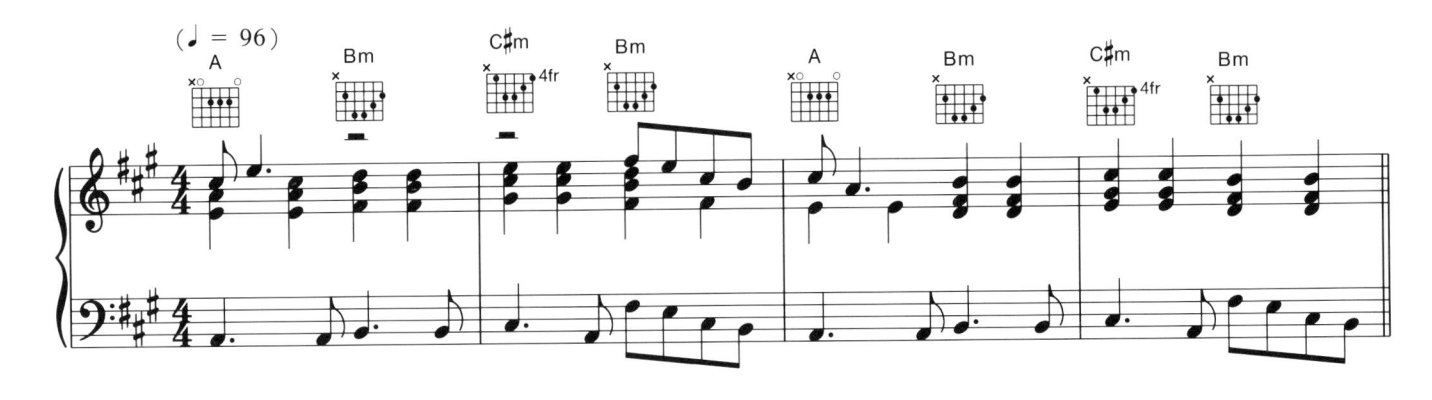

(♩ = 96)

Pull the string, and I'll wink at you,— I'm your pup-pet.
Pull an-oth-er string, and I'll kiss your lips,— I'm your pup-pet.

I'll do fun-ny things, if you want me to,— I'm your
Snap your fin-ger, and I'll turn you some flips I'm your

© 1966 Fame Publishing Co. Inc.
Warner Chappell Music Ltd., London W1Y 3FA

pup-pet.
pup-pet. I'm yours to have, and to hold
Your ev-ery wish is my com-mand,

dar - ling, you've got full con - trol of your pup-pet.
all you got-ta do is wig-gle your lit - tle hand, I'm your

pup-pet, I'm your

pup-pet. I'm just a toy, just a fun-ny boy,

that makes you laugh when you're blue._____ I'll be won-der-ful, do just what I'm told, I'll do a-ny-thing for you,_____ I'm your pup-pet, I'm your pup-pet.

Pull them lit-tle strings, and I'll sing you a song,_____ I'm your pup-pet,

oh_ ba - by, make me do right, or make me do wrong, I'm your pup-pet. Mmm, treat me good, and I'll do a-ny-thing, I'm_ just a pup-pet, and you hold my strings, I'm your pup-pet, yeah, I'm your pup-pet. Walk-ing, talk-ing, living, loving, puppet, I'm hanging on a string girl, I'll do anything now come on now, come on now, oh, I'm your puppet. Ooh, ah, walking, talking, living, loving, puppet, and I love you, ah, I'm a smiling happy face when you want to, oh, even make you happy when you're feeling blue.

Love Letters

Love letters straight from your heart
Keep us so near while apart
I'm not alone in the night
When I can have all the love you write

I memorize every line
And I kiss the name that you sign
And darling then I read again
Right from the start
Love letters straight from your heart

I memorize every line
And I kiss the name that you sign
And darling then I read again
Right from the start
Love letters straight from your heart

Love Letters

Music by VICTOR YOUNG
Lyrics by EDWARD HEYMAN

Love letters straight from your heart, keep us so near while a-part. I'm not a-lone in the night,

© 1945 Famous Music Corp.
Administered by Warner Chappell Music International Ltd., London W1Y 3FA

when I can have all the love you write. I memorize every line, and I kiss the name that you sign, and darling then

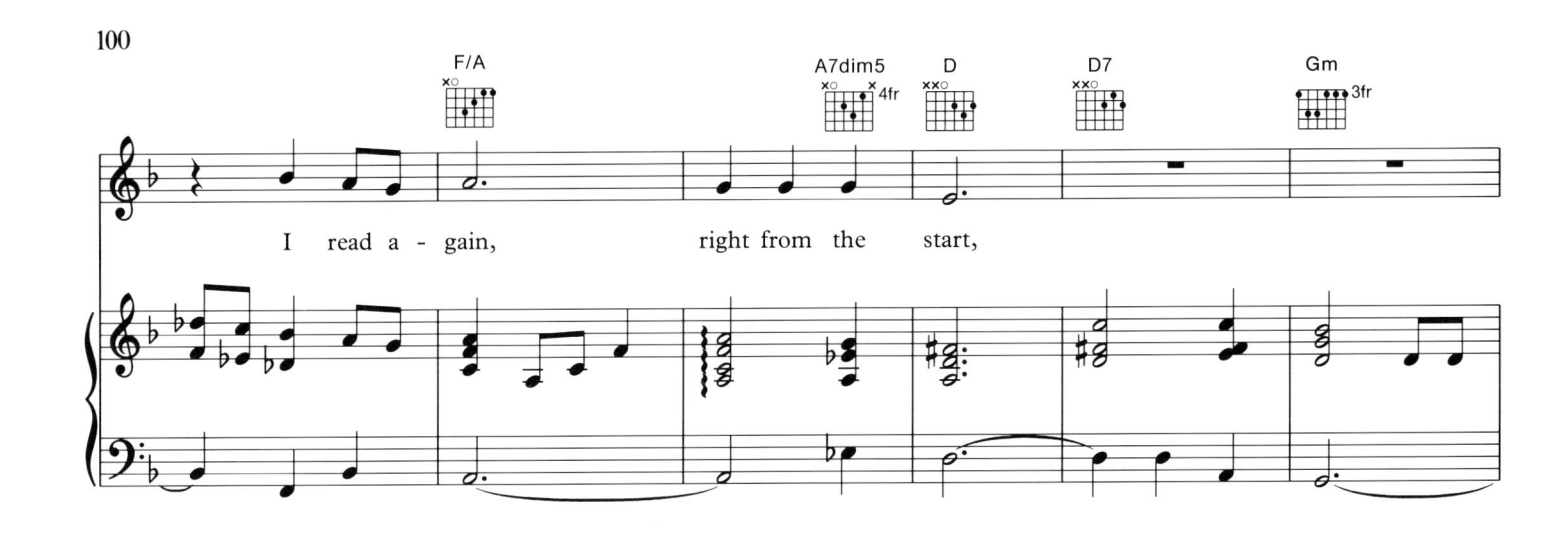

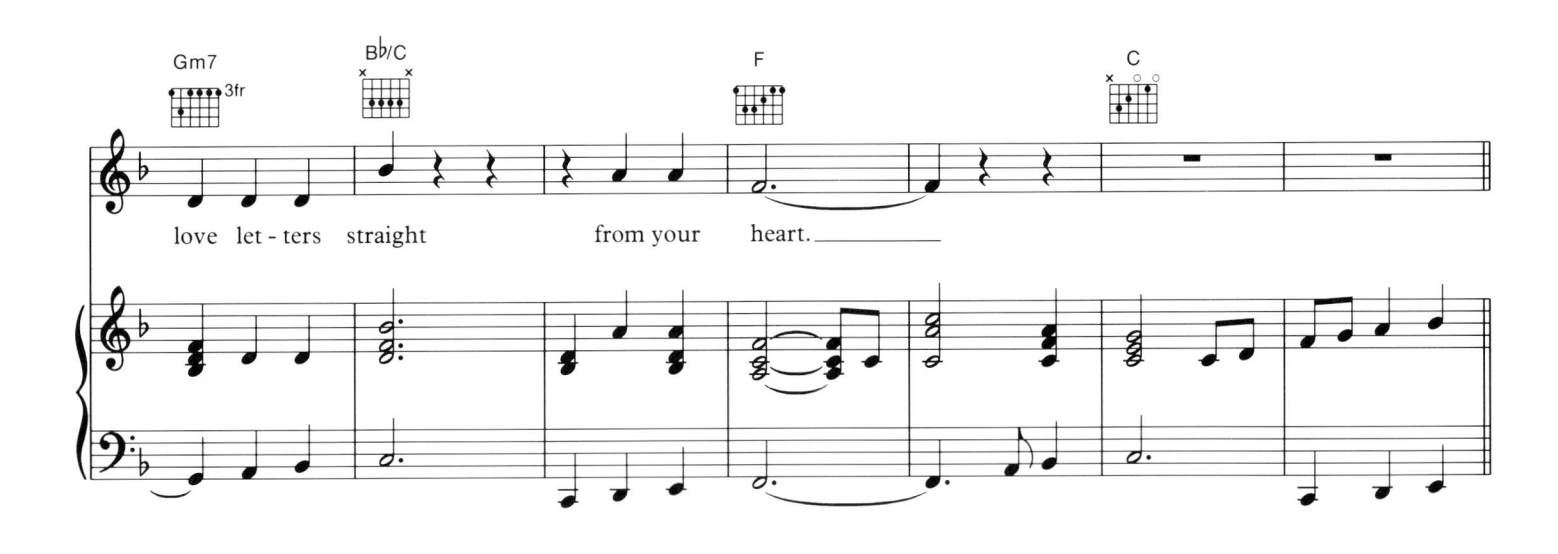

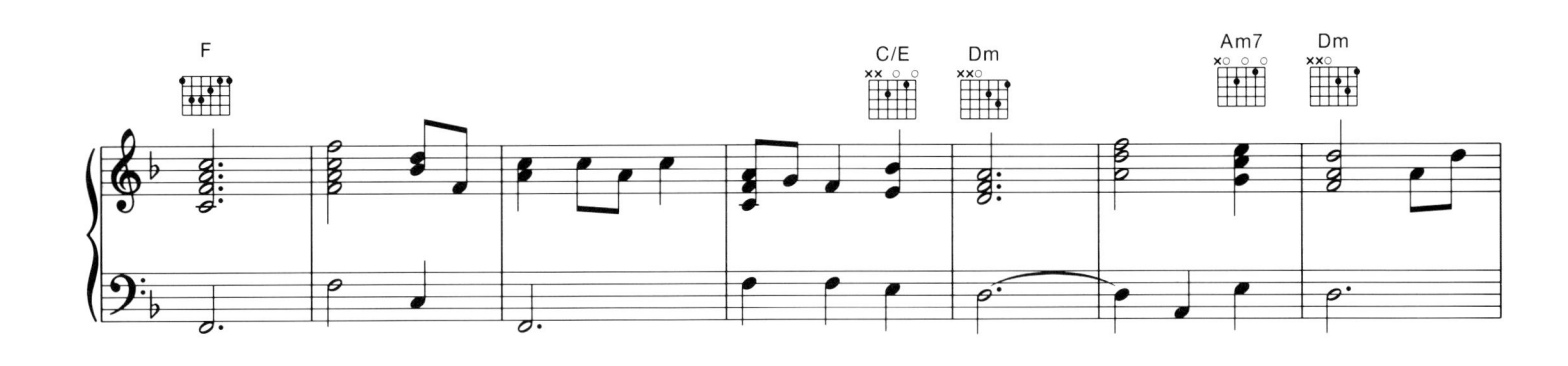

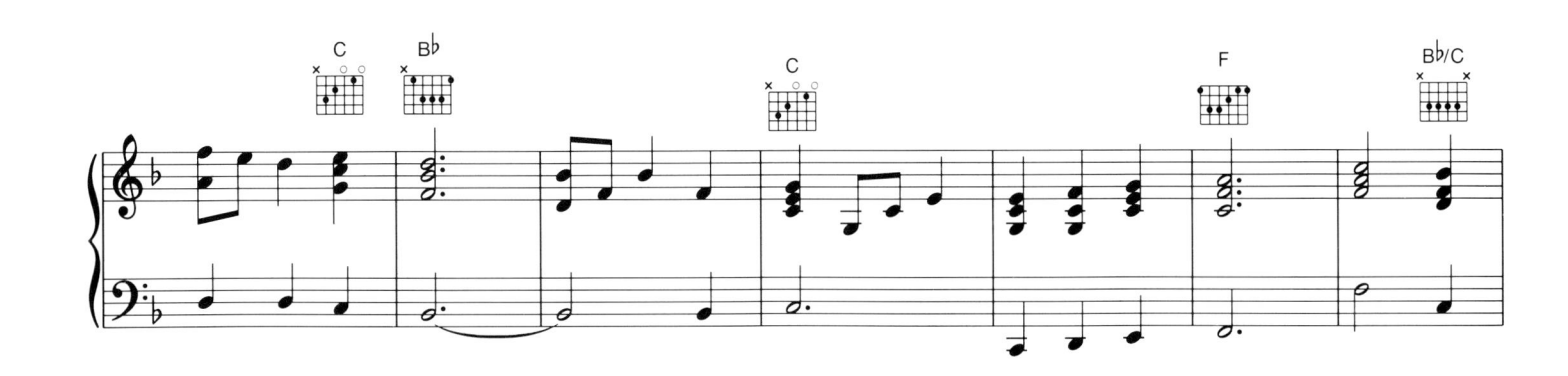

I read a - gain, right from the start, love let - ters straight from your heart.

101

I mem-or-ize____ ev-ery line,____

and I kiss the name that you sign,_

102

BORN TO LOSE

Born to lose I've lived my life in vain
Every dream has only brought me pain
All my life I've always been so blue
Born to lose and now I'm losing you

Born to lose oh it seems so hard to bear
When I wake and find that you're not there
You've grown tired and now you say we're through
I'm born to lose hey now I'm losing you

Born to lose I've lived my life in vain
(Lived my life in vain)
Every dream has only brought me pain
(Has only brought me pain)
All my life
(All my life)
I've always been so blue
(Been so blue)
Born to lose
(I'm born to lose)
And now I'm losing you
(I'm losing you)
Born to lose and now, Elton, I'm losing you

Born To Lose

Music & Lyrics by
TED DAFFAN

blue, born to lose, _____ and now

I'm los-ing you. Born to

lose, oh it seems so hard to bear,

when I wake, and find that you're not there.

Oh, you've grown tired, and now you say we're through, I'm born to lose, hey now I'm losing you.

Born to lose,

Lyrics:

I've lived my life in vain, (lived my life in vain,) ev-ery dream has on-ly brought me pain, (has on-ly brought me pain.) All my life, (all my life,) I've al-ways been so blue, (been so blue,) born to

A13 Em7 A13 Em/C♯ F♯7 Bm7
lose, (I'm born to lose,) and now I'm los-ing you, (I'm___ los-ing you,)_
E7add♯4 Bm/G♯7 A7 Em9 A7♭9
___ born to lose, and now El-ton, I'm los-ing
D6 D7 G7 A♭6add 9 G♭6aug5 E6add 9 D6add 9
you.
C6add 9 B♭6add 9 G/A E♭7/A D13add♯4

Don't Let The Sun Go Down On Me

I can't light no more of your darkness
All my pictures seem to fade to black and white
I'm growing tired and time stands still before me
Frozen here on the ladder of my life

It's much too late to save myself from falling
I took a chance and changed your way of life
But you misread my meaning when I met you
Closed the door and left me blinded by the light

Don't let the sun go down on me
Although I searched myself
It's always someone else I see
I'd just allow a fragment of your life to wander free
But losing everything is like the sun going down on me

I can't find oh the right romantic line
But see me once and see the way I feel
Don't discard me just because you think I mean you harm
But these cuts I have, oh they need love to help them heal

Don't let the sun go down on me
Although I searched myself
It's always someone else I see
I'd just allow a fragment of your life to wander free
But losing everything is like the sun going down on me

1985

Don't Let The Sun Go Down On Me

Music by ELTON JOHN
Lyrics by BERNIE TAUPIN

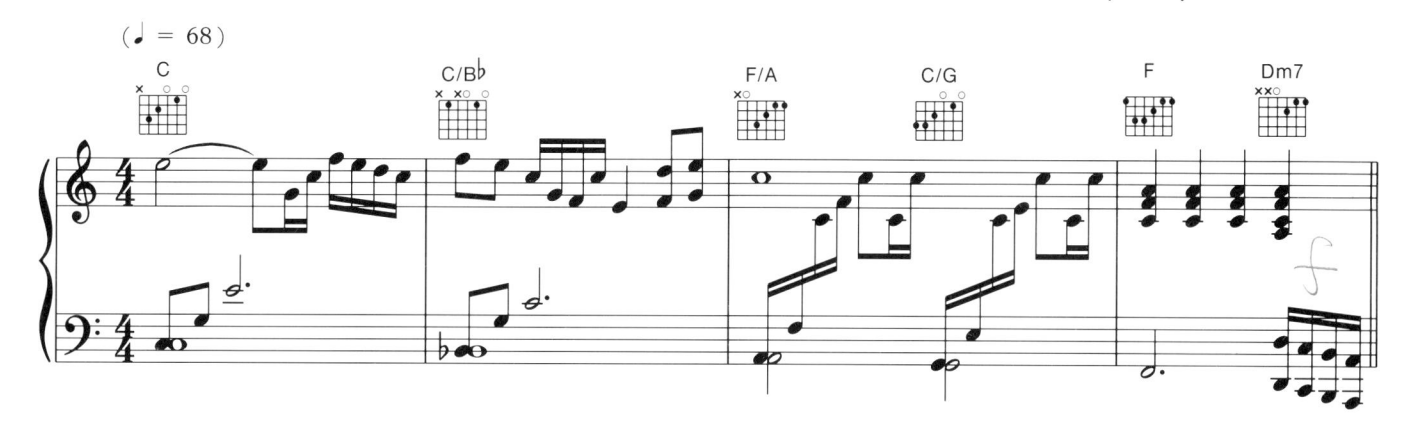

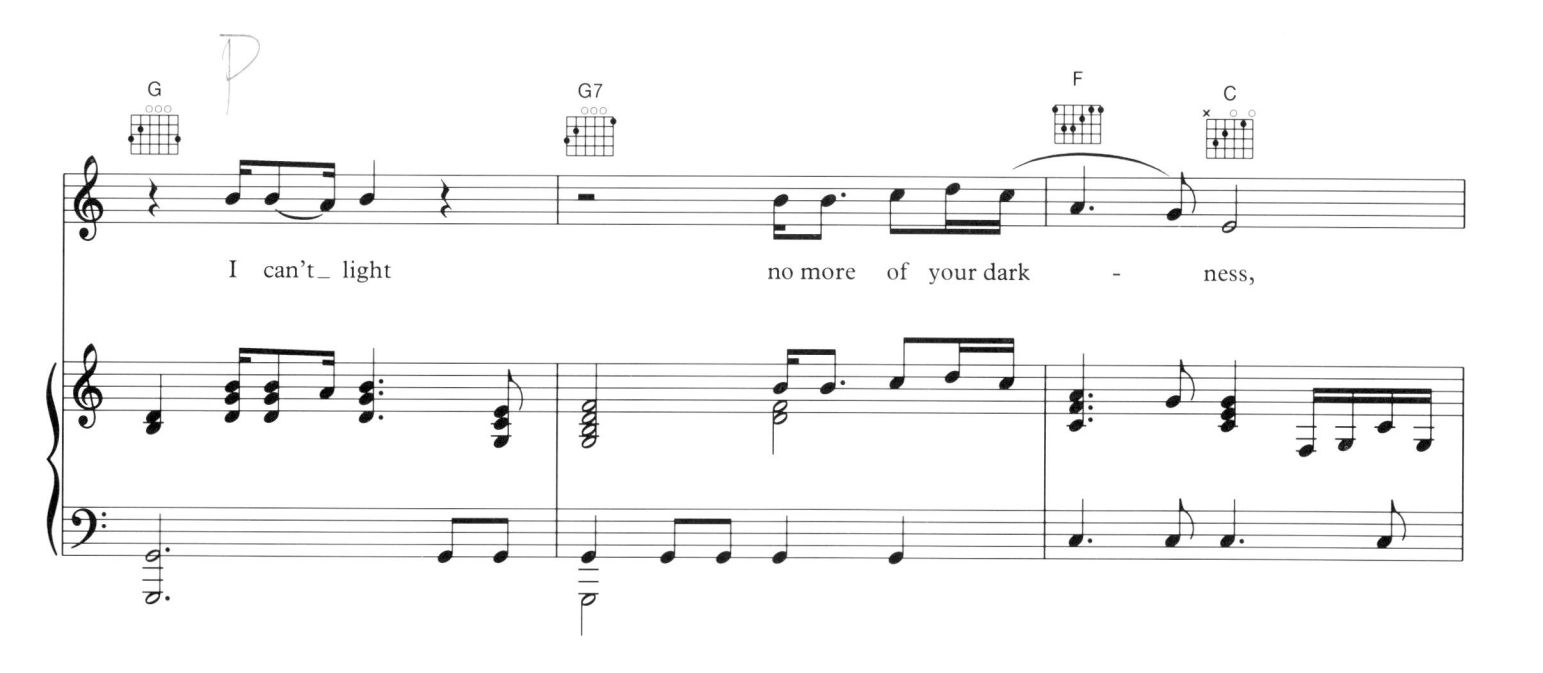

I can't light no more of your darkness, all my pictures seem to fade to black and white.

© 1974 Happenstance Ltd./Rouge Booze Inc.
Administered by Warner Chappell Music Ltd., London W1Y 3FA

I'm growing tired, and time stands still before me, frozen here on the ladder of my life. It's much too late to save myself from falling,

C
C7/E
F
B♭/F
F
I took a chance, and changed your way of life,
G
C/G
G
G7
but you mis-read my mean-ing when I
F/C
C
C/E
F
met you,
closed the door,
extra notes
C/G
G
F/G
and left me blind - ed by the light.
Cresc
TURN OVER

Don't let the sun go down on me, although I searched myself, it's always someone else I see, I'd just allow a fragment of your life to wander free, but losing everything is like the sun going down on me.

Go Down On Me

Music by ELTON JOHN
Lyrics by BERNIE TAUPIN

I can't light no more of your darkness,

all my pictures seem to fade to black and white.

© 1974 Happenstance Ltd./Rouge Booze Inc.
Administered by Warner Chappell Music Ltd., London W1Y 3FA

I'm growing tired, and time stands still before me, frozen here on the ladder of my life. It's much too late to save myself from falling,

F/A
C/G
F
G
I can't find,
G7
C
C/E
oh the right ro - man-tic line,
F
G7
C/G
but see me once,
and see the way I feel.
G7
C/G
G7
DON'T TURN
Don't dis-card me
just be-cause you think

C
C/E
F
I mean you harm,
but these cuts I have,
D.S. al Coda
C/G
G
G7
oh they need love to help them heal.
CODA
C
C/B♭
F/A
A♭
B♭
4fr
me.
C
C/B♭
Am7
Don't let the sun go down on me,
al-though I searched my-self, it's al-ways

C
C/E
F
I mean you harm,
but these cuts I have
3
D.𝄋 al Co
C/G
G
G7
oh they need love to help them heal.

I can't find,

oh the right ro - man-tic line,

some-one else I see, I'd just al-low a frag-ment of your life to wan-der free, but los-ing ev-ery-thing is like the sun go-ing down on me.

DUETS FOR ONE

Look at you
Could I have been so foolish and so green
A face that smiles at every passing scene?
Look at you
You're lost behind a web of woven time
When each emotion pin-balled on your mind
Look at me
I'm happy now I see your face and smile
I watch the judge and jury at your trial
Look at me
I know the road ahead will twist and turn
Now I have a time to stand and learn
That you and I have come so far with a shaken faith
From the pit of a broken heart
To a feeling great
Feel like life has just begun
No more singing duets for one

I hold your picture here beside my bed
You had a party raging in your head
Look at me
I look at you with vacancy and hurt
And here today all I can do is learn
Look at me
I'm happy now I see your face and smile
I watch the judge and jury at your trial
Look at me
I know the road ahead will twist and turn
Now I have the time to stand and learn
That you and I have come so far with a shaken faith
From the pit of a broken heart
To a feeling great
Feel like life has just begun
No more singing duets for one

I have this picture of me looking at you
Looking at me
And I would like to say goodbye sweet memory
Oh you and I have come so far with a shaken faith
From the pit of a broken heart
To a feeling great
Feel like life has just begun
No more singing duets for one
No more singing duets for one
No more singing duets for one

Duets For One

Music by ELTON JOHN
Lyrics by CHRISTOPHER DIFFORD

(♩ = 92)

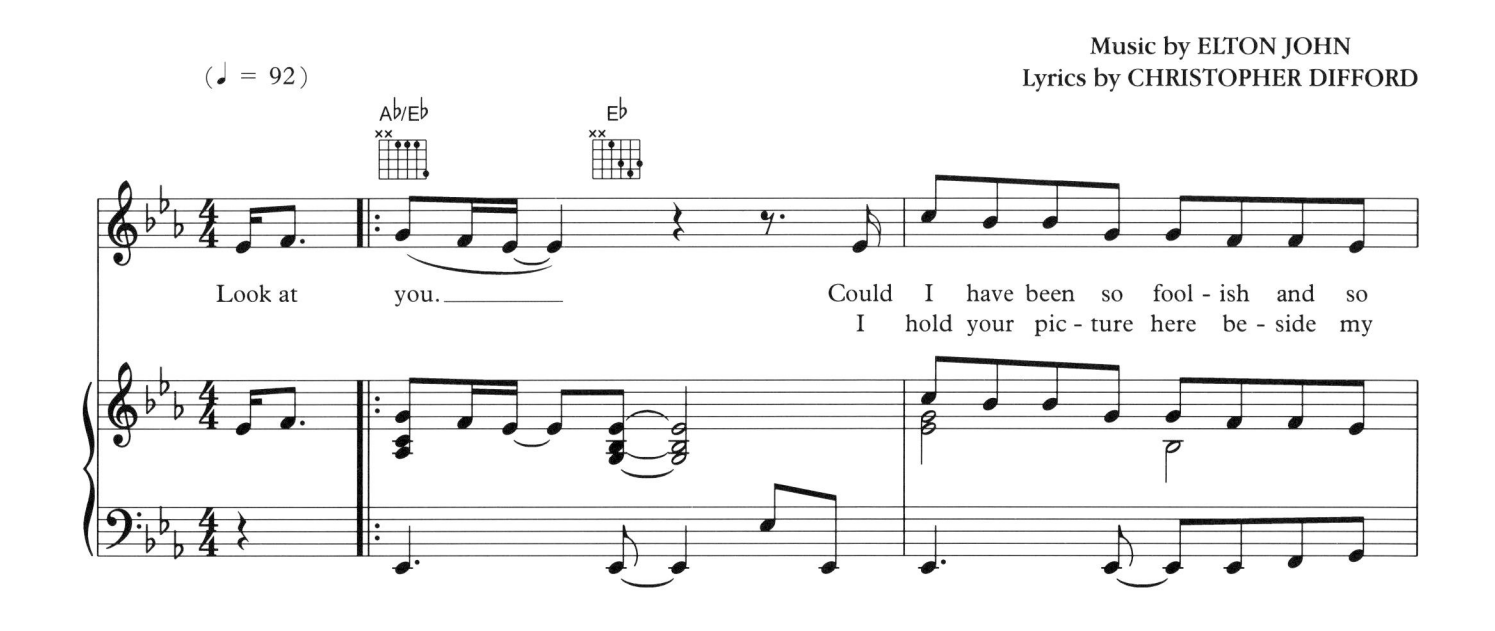

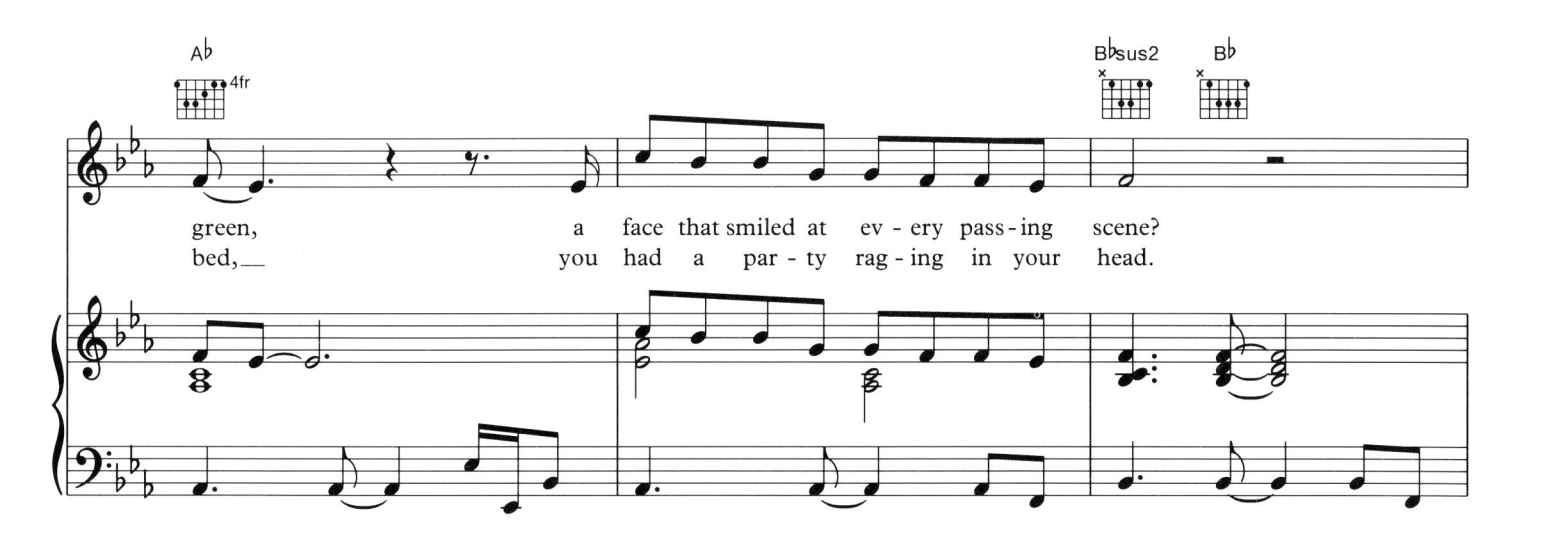

Look at you. Could I have been so foolish and so green, a face that smiled at every passing scene?

I hold your picture here beside my bed, you had a party raging in your head.

Look at you. You're lost behind a web of woven
Look at me. I look at you with vacancy and

© 1993 William A. Bong Ltd./Warner Chappell Music Ltd., London W1Y 3FA/
EMI Virgin Music Ltd., London WC2H 0EA

time,
hurt,

when each e-mo-tion pin-balled on your mind.
and here to-day all I can do is learn.

Look at me. I'm hap-py now, I see your face and smile, I watch the judge and ju-ry at your trial.

Look at me. I know the road a-head will twist and

turn, now I have a time__ to stand and learn__ that you and__ I_____ have come so far__ with a sha-ken faith__ from the pit of a bro- -ken heart,_ to a feel-ing great,_

122

Lyrics:
feel like life has just be-gun, no more sing-ing du-ets for one. I have this pic-ture of me look-ing at you, look-ing at me,

A♭5
4fr
Fm
and I would like to say good - bye sweet
G7
D.𝄋 al Coda
me - mo - ry. Oh, you and I
CODA
Fm
C/E Dm/F C/G Dm/A Cmaj7/G Dm/G C
No more sing - ing du - ets for one,
Fm C/E Dm/F C/G Dm/A Cmaj7/G Dm/G C
no more sing - ing du - ets for one.

Printed in England
Panda Press · Haverhill · Suffolk • 5/94